HAPPY THANKSGIVING!
THINGS TO MAKE AND DO

Written by Judith Conaway
Illustrated by Renzo Barto

Troll Associates

Library of Congress Cataloging in Publication Data

Conaway, Judith, (date)
    Happy Thanksgiving! Things to make and do.

    Summary: Provides instructions for making Indian
cutouts, place mats, Indian cornbread, and other
Thanksgiving decorations and foods, as well as
descriptions of two games.
    1. Thanksgiving decorations—Juvenile literature.
2. Thanksgiving cookery—Juvenile literature.
[1. Thanksgiving decorations. 2. Thanksgiving cookery.
3. Handicraft. 4. Cookery, American] I. Barto,
Renzo, ill. II. Title.
TT900.T5C66   1986   745.594'1   85-16463
ISBN 0-8167-0668-9 (lib. bdg.)
ISBN 0-8167-0669-7 (pbk.)

CONTENTS

Thanksgiving is a special day. It's a time for friends, family, and lots of fun. It's also a time for giving thanks—just as the Indians and Pilgrims did long ago on the first Thanksgiving. Here are some Thanksgiving things to make and do. They'll add to the fun of your holiday!

BIRCH-BARK EAGLE

At the time of the first Thanksgiving, the Indians made cutouts like these from birch bark, using stone knives. You can make the same toys with paper and scissors.

Here's what you need:

 Scissors

 Black crayon

Ruler

Construction paper

Here's what you do:

1. Draw short lines on the construction paper to make it look like birch bark. Use a ruler and black crayon.

2. Fold a piece of "birch-bark" paper in half and copy the eagle pattern (shown on the next page) onto it. The dotted line of the pattern should line up with the fold in the construction paper.

3. Cut out the eagle shape and unfold it. Your eagle is ready to fly!

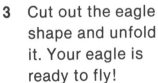

MORE INDIAN CUTOUTS

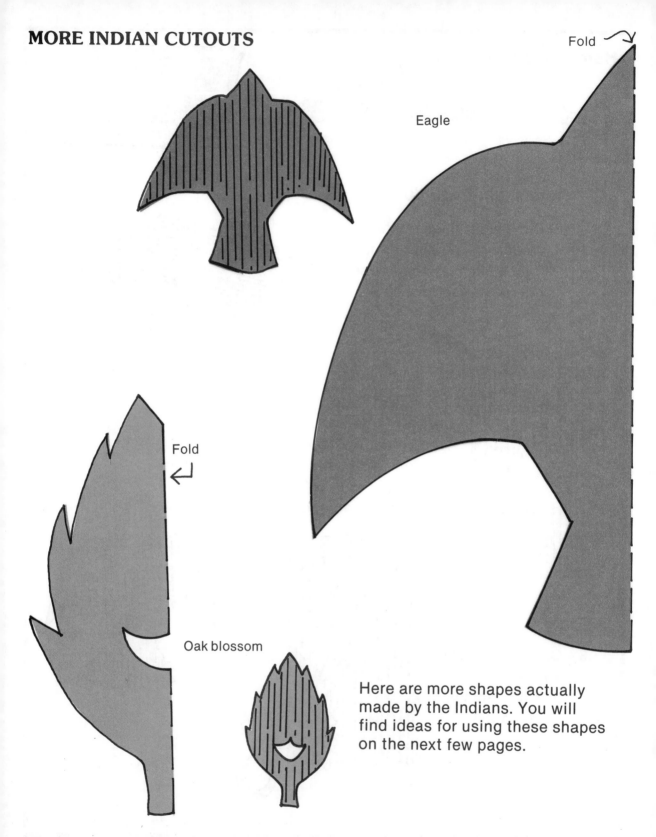

Fold ⤵

Eagle

Fold
←

Oak blossom

Here are more shapes actually made by the Indians. You will find ideas for using these shapes on the next few pages.

6

Fold

Turtle

Two in a canoe

Fold

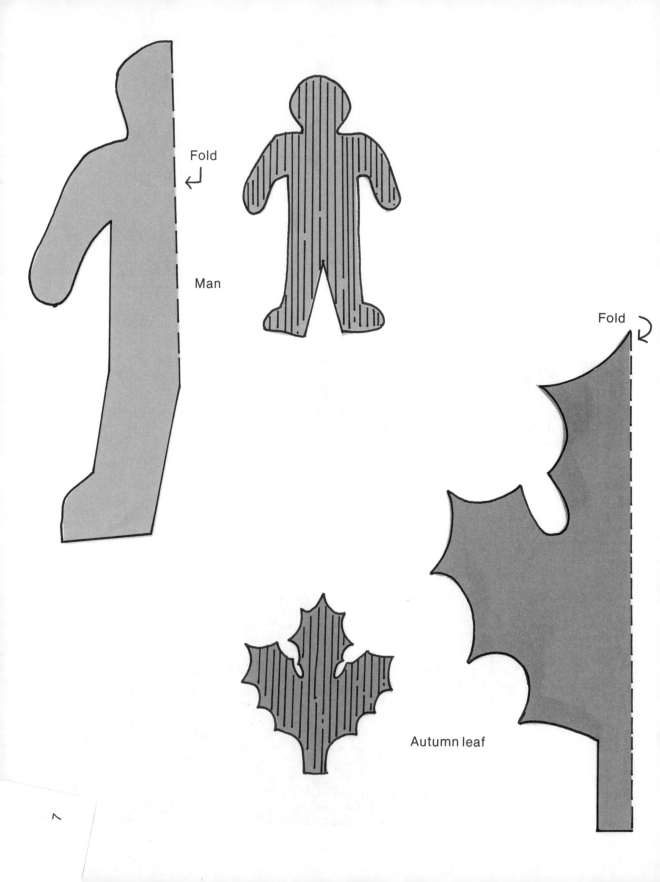

Fold

Man

Fold

Autumn leaf

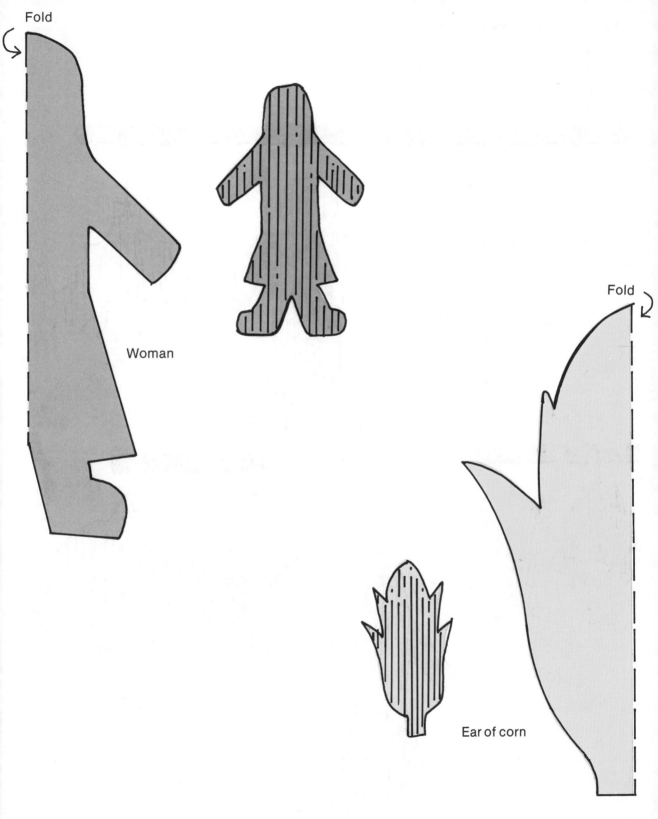

Fold

Woman

Ear of corn

Fold

9

THANKSGIVING MOBILE

Use the birch-bark cutouts to make this great Thanksgiving decoration. Directions for making the cutouts are on pages 4-9.

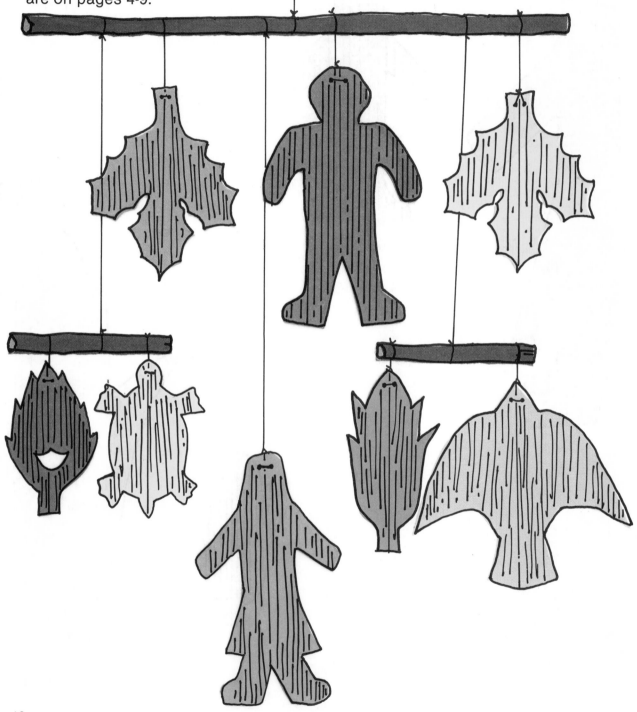

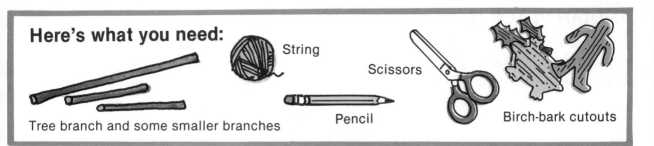

Here's what you need:

Tree branch and some smaller branches

String

Pencil

Scissors

Birch-bark cutouts

Here's what you do:

1 Using a pencil point, carefully punch two holes near the top of each cutout.

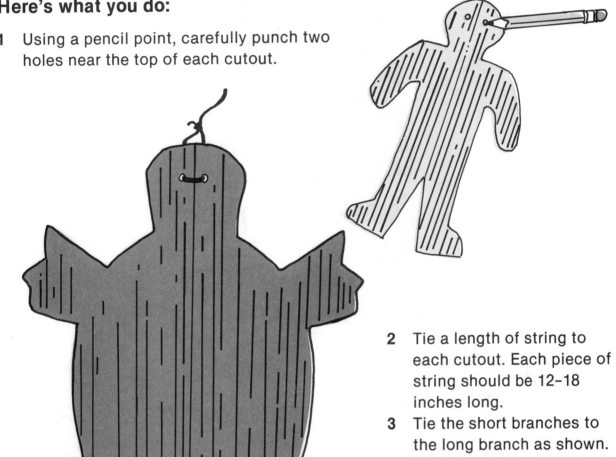

2 Tie a length of string to each cutout. Each piece of string should be 12–18 inches long.

3 Tie the short branches to the long branch as shown.

4 Tie some cutouts to the short branches and tie the other cutouts to the long branch.

5 Attach another piece of string to the long branch and hang your mobile up!

11

INDIAN PLACE MATS

The Indians used birch-bark cutouts as patterns for art. Why not decorate your Thanksgiving table the Indian way with these pretty place mats? Turn to pages 4–9 for directions on how to make the cutouts.

Here's what you need:

Crayons or markers

Large sheets of construction paper

Birch-bark cutouts

Here's what you do:

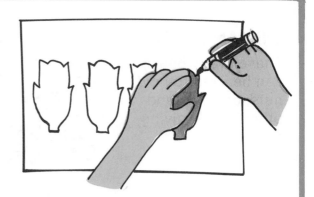

1   For each place mat, you will need one sheet of paper. Lay the paper flat on a table. Put a cutout near one edge. Trace around the cutout.

2   Place the cutout next to your first shape. Trace again and again to make a repeat design. Color in some of the shapes.

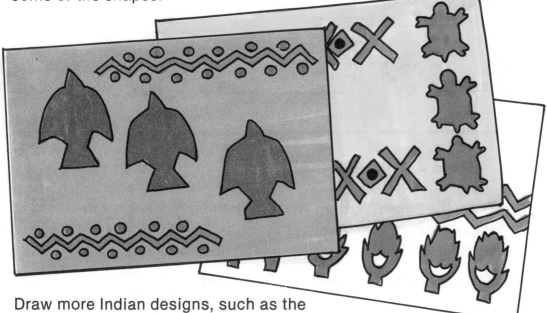

3   Draw more Indian designs, such as the circles, crosses, and zigzag lines shown here.

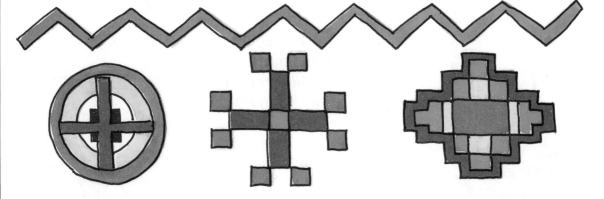

INDIAN BASKET

These pretty baskets can be used to hold nuts, candies, and other Thanksgiving treats.

Here's what you need:

Pencil

Scissors

Paints and brush

Twine

Colored construction paper

Tape

Here's what you do:

1 Copy the basket pattern (shown on the opposite page) onto a sheet of construction paper. Cut this shape out.

2 Gently fold the four sides of the basket up.

3 Fold points A and B together, as shown. Secure all three parts with a piece of tape. Repeat this step for opposite sides C and D.

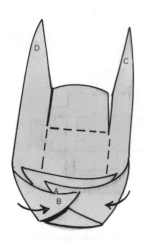

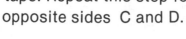

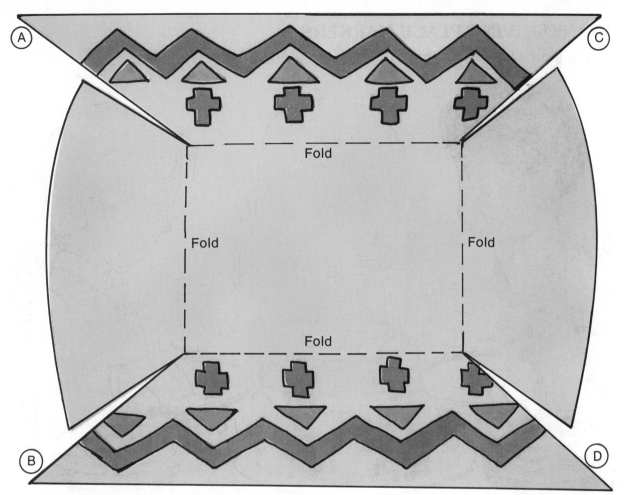

Fold

Fold

Fold

Fold

4 Using a pencil point, carefully make a hole through the tape and three layers of paper. Repeat for the other side.

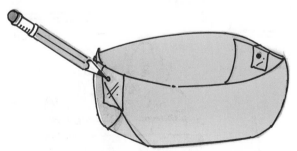

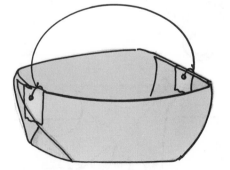

5 To make the handle, tie a length of twine to each hole.

6 If you like, paint Indian designs on your basket.

THANKSGIVING PLACE MARKERS

Here's a nice way to brighten up your table on Thanksgiving day.

Here's what you need:

Scissors

Construction paper

Crayons

Ruler

Pencil

Here's what you do:

1 Mark off as many 3-inch squares as you need on a sheet of construction paper. (Each square makes one place marker.) Then cut them apart.

2 Using your ruler and pencil, lightly mark off the center fold line.

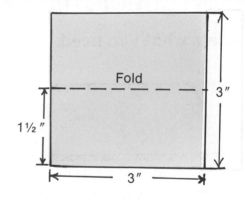

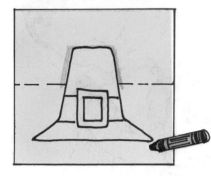

3 Copy any of the designs below onto the squares.

4 Cut around the top part of the design where outlined in red. Color in the design.

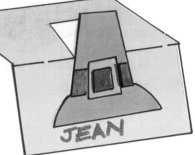

5 Now carefully fold the square in half so the place marker can stand up.

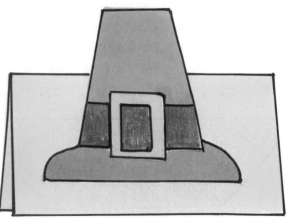

6 Write your guest's name on the place marker.

INDIAN FEATHERED HEADBAND

Here's what you need:

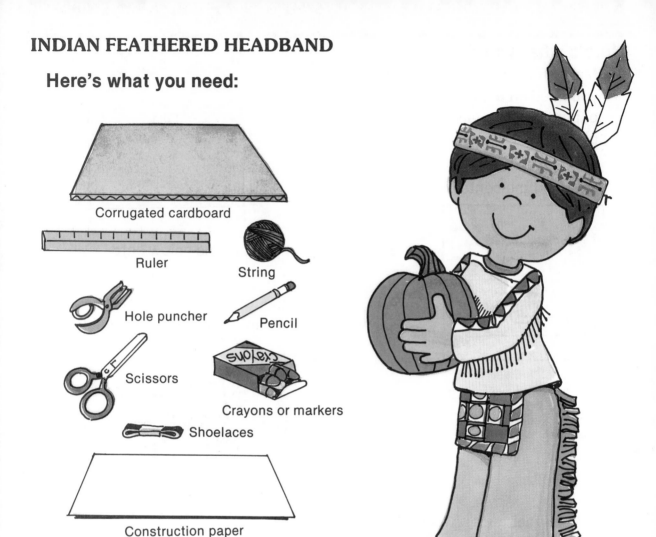

Corrugated cardboard

Ruler

String

Hole puncher

Pencil

Scissors

Crayons or markers

Shoelaces

Construction paper

For the feathers, here's what you do:

1   Cut strips of construction paper that are about 2 inches wide and
    6½ inches long. Fold the construction paper in half lengthwise and
    copy the feather pattern shown here onto it. The fold of the paper
    should line up with the dotted line.
2   Cut out the feathers. With crayons, add some color and details.

For the headband, here's what you do:

1 Use string to measure the distance around your head. Cut a strip of cardboard 2 inches wide and as long as the string.

Be sure to cut across the ridges of the cardboard, as shown.

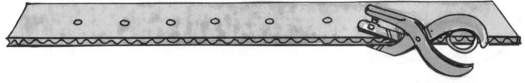

2 Punch holes along the middle of the cardboard strip. Make the holes about an inch apart. Punch an *even* number of holes.

3 Thread a shoelace in and out of the holes. Draw Indian designs on the headband.

4 Stick feathers in between the cardboard ridges of the headband. To wear the headband, tie it around your head.

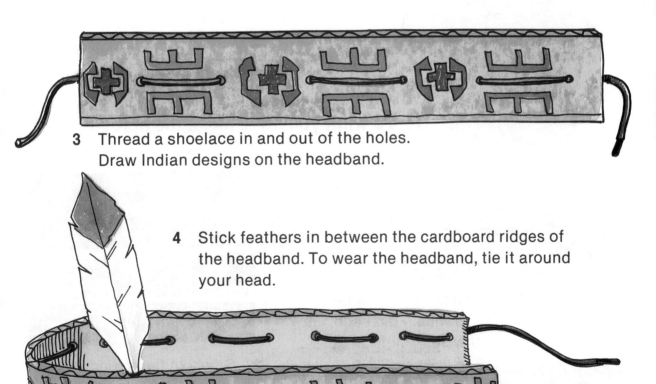

PILGRIM BUCKLE BELT

It's fun to dress up as a Pilgrim on Thanksgiving. Here's a Pilgrim buckle belt to add to your costume.

Here's what you need:

Black construction paper

Gold tag board or yellow construction paper

Glue

Scissors

Pencil

Ruler

Here's what you do to make the belt:

1 Cut 4 long strips of black construction paper, each 3 inches wide. Fold each piece in half lengthwise.

3"

2 Glue 2 of the folded strips together, as shown.

3 Now glue the other 2 strips together.

Here's what you do to make the buckle:

1 Fold a 6-inch square of gold tag board in half.

2 Copy the 2 patterns shown here onto the folded tag board.

3 Cut out the 2 pieces.

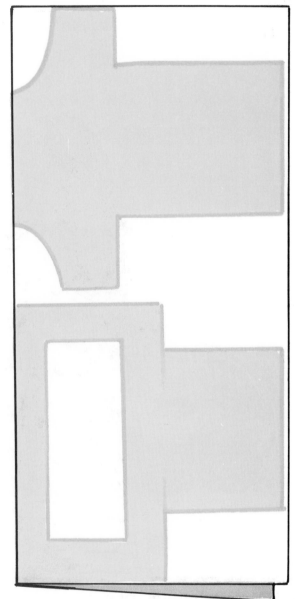

4 Glue buckle parts to the belt. Let dry.

5 For a good fit, hook the buckle parts together. Then wrap the belt around your waist. With the buckle at your back, make a pencil mark where the 2 pieces overlap. Glue the 2 lengths together at that mark.

6 Let glue dry completely. Your new Pilgrim belt is ready to wear.

TOY CANOE

Here's what you need:

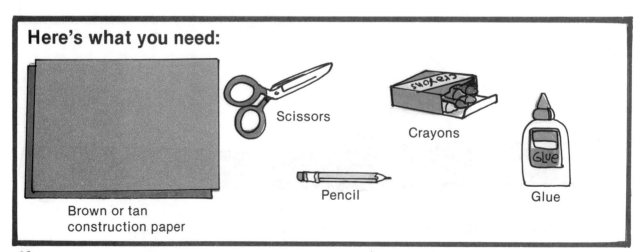

Scissors

Crayons

Glue

Pencil

Brown or tan
construction paper

Here's what you do:

1 Use a half sheet of construction paper to make one canoe. Fold the half sheet in half like this.

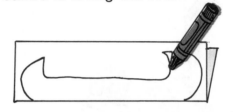

2 Copy the canoe pattern. Draw the shape so that the bottom of the canoe is along the fold.

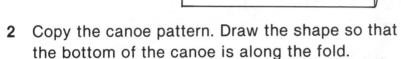

3 Cut out the canoe and draw Indian designs on it with your crayons.

4 Open the canoe and lay it flat, with the inside facing up. Put a thin line of glue on the curved ends, as shown, and press the ends together.

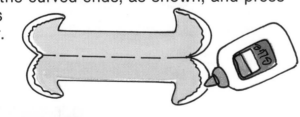

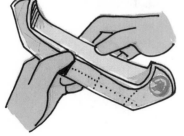

5 When the glue has dried, gently open the canoe.

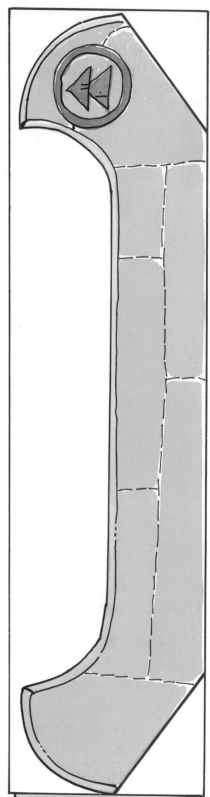

MINIATURE *MAYFLOWER*

This is how to make a small model of the *Mayflower,* the ship that carried the Pilgrims to America.

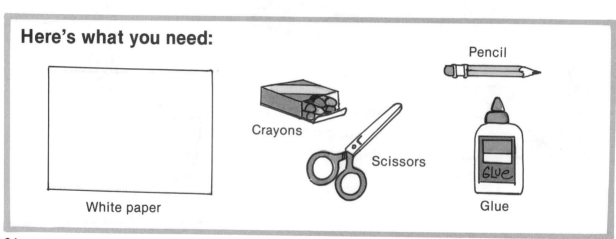

Here's what you need:

White paper

Crayons

Scissors

Pencil

Glue

Turn the page for more
directions.

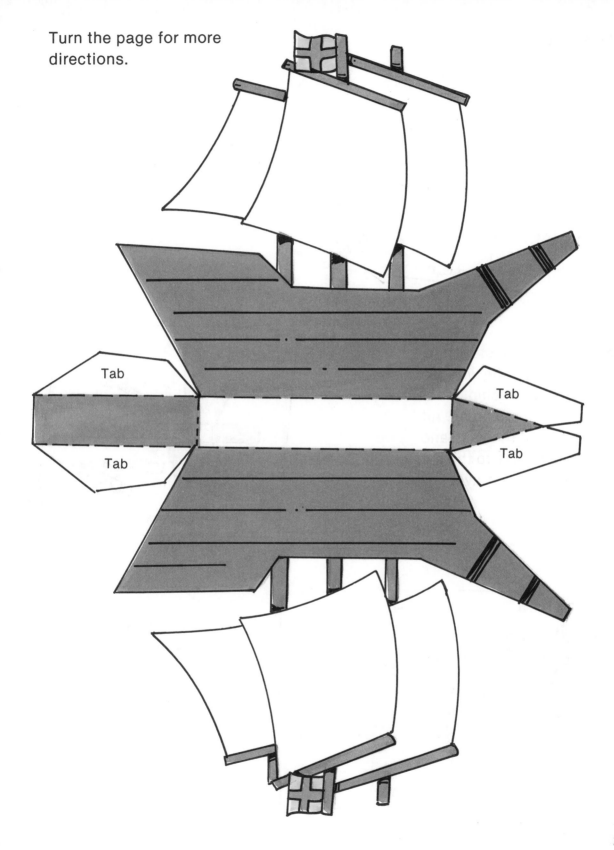

Here's what you do:

1 Carefully copy the outline of the ship onto a sheet of white paper. Use the pattern shown on page 25.

2 Use a brown crayon to color in all the wooden parts of the ship. Do not color the tab areas. Add details of the sails and some planks to the ship with a black crayon.

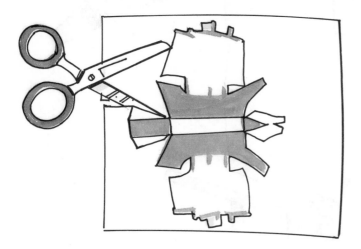

3 Carefully cut out the ship.

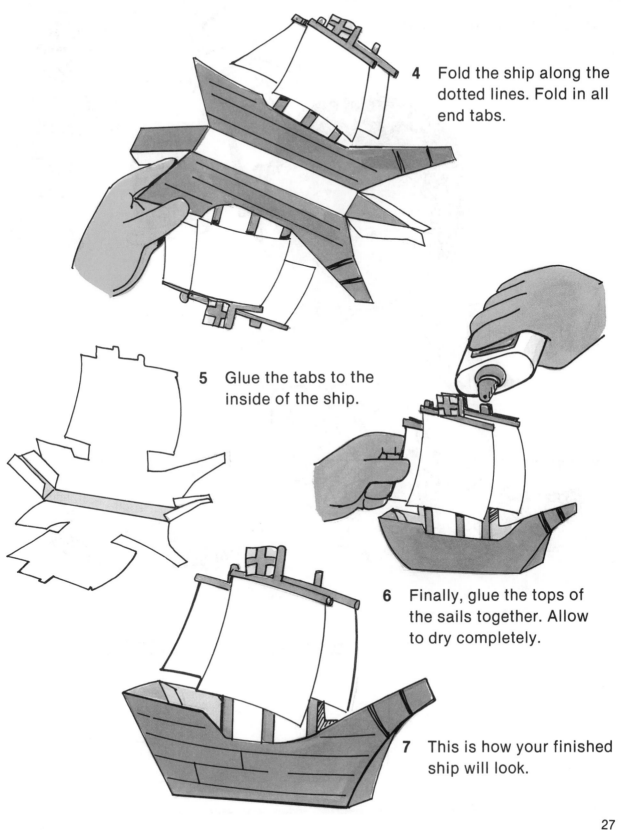

4 Fold the ship along the dotted lines. Fold in all end tabs.

5 Glue the tabs to the inside of the ship.

6 Finally, glue the tops of the sails together. Allow to dry completely.

7 This is how your finished ship will look.

PILGRIM-INDIAN CHAIN

Here's what you need:

Construction paper

Pencil

Crayons

Scissors

Tape

Here's what you do:

1 Copy the Pilgrim and Indian patterns shown on the next two pages onto construction paper.

Make four people for every foot of chain that you want.

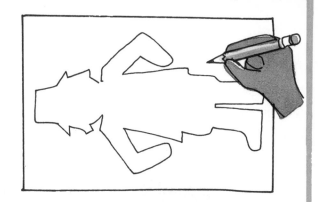

2 Draw faces and clothes on the people and color them.

3 Cut out the figures.

4 Link the arms of the people to make a chain. Turn the figures over and tape the arms together.

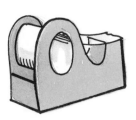

Indian woman

Pilgrim man

Pilgrim woman

Indian brave

THANKSGIVING LEAF-RUBBING CARDS

Your family and friends will love to receive these pretty Thanksgiving cards. They're made by using autumn leaves, and inside each card, you can write your very own message!

Here's what you need:

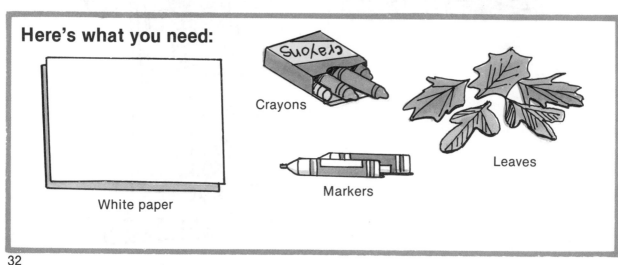

White paper

Crayons

Markers

Leaves

Here's what you do:

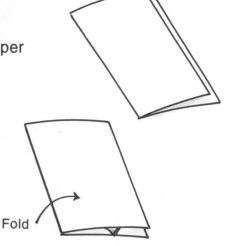

1 For each card, fold a sheet of paper in half like this.

Fold

2 Place one or two leaves inside each card and close the card. Using a crayon, lightly rub across the front of the card in the area where the leaf is. The outline and patterns of the leaf will appear. (*Note:* you can vary your design by using two or more leaves.)

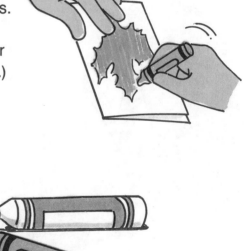

3 Remove the leaf from inside the card. Use another color crayon or your markers to decorate the background. You can use some of the ideas shown here—or better yet, create some designs of your own.

4 Open the card and write a special Thanksgiving message inside.

PAPER-CUP TEPEE

Here's what you need:

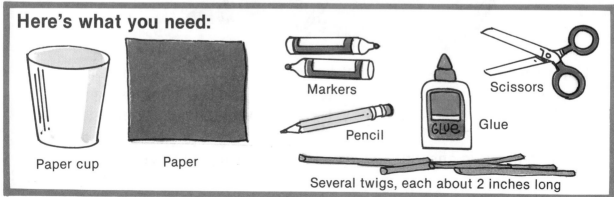

Paper cup

Paper

Markers

Pencil

Glue

Scissors

Several twigs, each about 2 inches long

Here's what you do: **1** Trace the outline of the wide end of the cup onto a piece of paper.

2 Cut out the circle you have traced. This will be the floor of your tepee.

3 Copy this door pattern onto the cup. Make one cut, as shown, and fold back.

4 Cut out the narrow end of the cup.

5 Apply glue around the edge of the wide end of the cup, as shown. Glue the cup to the paper circle. Let dry.

6 Draw designs on the outside of the cup with your markers.

7 Put a spot of glue at the end of each twig and glue to the inside of the cup like this. Your tepee is ready!

OLD ENGLISH "SALLET"

Here's how to make a great "sallet," or salad as we call it today.
The recipe comes from a very old book, widely read by the Pilgrims.

Here's what you need:

Cucumber

Raw spinach

Lettuce

Cabbage

Onion

Raisins

Mint

Sage

Walnuts

Almonds

Raspberries

Measuring cup and spoons

Sugar

Small bowl

Spoon

Oil and vinegar

Chopping board and knife

Salad bowl, fork, and spoon

Colander

Here's what you do:

1 Peel off enough leaves of spinach, lettuce, and cabbage to fill about half of your salad bowl. Wash and drain the leaves well in the colander.

2 Toss all the green leaves together. Add shredded sage and mint. Then add the raisins and raspberries. Toss again.

1 Cucumber

1 Onion

3 Chop the onion, cucumber, walnuts, and almonds. Add them to the salad. *Note:* If you're not allowed to use a knife by yourself, ask a grownup for help.

½ Cup raisins

¼ Cup raspberries

¼ Cup chopped walnuts

¼ Cup chopped almonds

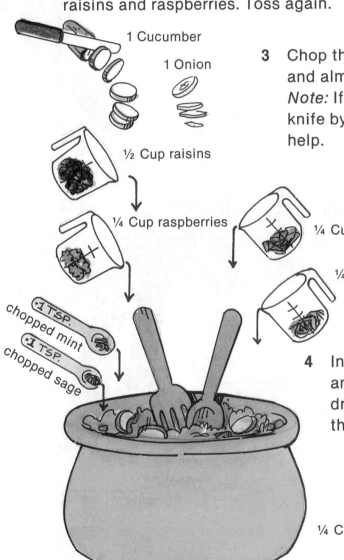

·1 TSP. chopped mint

·1 TSP. chopped sage

4 In a small bowl, mix the sugar, oil, and vinegar. Mix well. Add this dressing to the salad and toss for the last time.

½ Cup oil

¼ Cup sugar

½ Cup vinegar

MAPLE-NUT-BERRY POPCORN BALLS

Here's what you need:

Walnuts

Raspberries or blueberries

Maple syrup

Popcorn

Butter

Plate

Wooden spoon

Large bowl

Here's what you do:

1 Put enough popcorn to feed your guests into a big bowl. Add some chopped walnuts and berries. Add some melted butter. (*Note:* If you are not allowed to use a stove by yourself, ask a grownup for help.) Stir the mixture with a wooden spoon.

2 Pour maple syrup over the warm popcorn. Stir until all the corn, nuts, and berries are covered.

3 Shape the sticky corn into balls and place on a plate. Put the balls into the refrigerator until the syrup hardens, then eat!

INDIAN CORNBREAD

This delicious cornbread makes a fine addition to any Thanksgiving feast.

Here's what you need:

Spatula

Spoon

Frying pan

Pot holder

Cornmeal

Cooking oil

Milk

Salt

Mixing bowl

Measuring cup and spoons

Here's what you do:

1   Mix the cornmeal and salt in the bowl.

2   Add the milk and 1 teaspoon of cooking oil to the mixture. Stir well.

1 Cup cornmeal

1 Tsp. salt

½ Cup milk

1 Tsp. oil

3   Pour 3 tablespoons of oil into the bottom of the frying pan. Using a pot holder, tilt the pan so that the whole bottom is covered with oil. Set the pan over a medium flame.

Note: If you are not allowed to use a stove by yourself, ask a grownup for help.

4   When the oil is hot, drop a spoonful of batter into the pan. When cooked, flip it over and brown on other side, like a pancake. Repeat until all the batter is gone.

THANKSGIVING SPORTS MATCH

The first Thanksgiving lasted for three days. In between the many feasts, the Pilgrims and Indians challenged each other to games, races, and wrestling matches. Here are some games you can play at your own Thanksgiving sports match.

STONE TOSS GAME

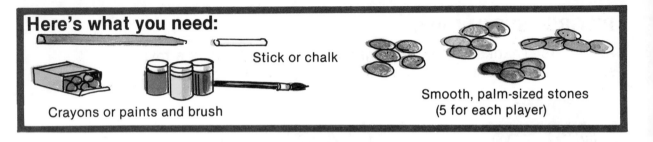

Here's what you need:

Stick or chalk

Crayons or paints and brush

Smooth, palm-sized stones
(5 for each player)

Here's what you do:

1   Each player is assigned a number. Use crayon or paints to mark each player's stones with his or her number.

2   To play the game, draw a circle on the ground outside. You can use chalk on pavement or just use a stick to draw a circle in the dirt. Take turns tossing the stones into the circle. Try to knock the other players' stones out. The game ends when all the stones have been tossed. The player with the most stones left in the circle wins the game.

Note: Always play safely! Make sure there's plenty of room around your play area and remember not to toss the stones in the direction of people or breakable objects.

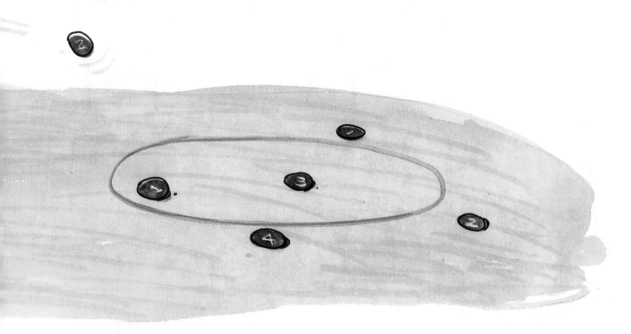

PILGRIM SPOONBALL

At the first Thanksgiving, the Pilgrims taught the Indians a favorite sport called spoonball. Spoonball was an early form of croquet.

Here's what you need:

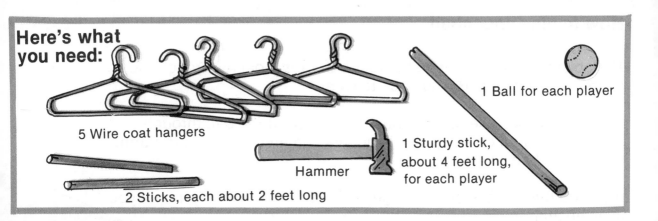

5 Wire coat hangers

2 Sticks, each about 2 feet long

Hammer

1 Sturdy stick, about 4 feet long, for each player

1 Ball for each player

Here's what you do:

1 Measure off the playing field. It can be any size you like. Drive a stick into the ground for a goal post at each end of the field.

2 Ask a grownup to help you unwind and straighten each coat hanger. Bend each one into an arch.

3 Push each arch into the ground. Make sure the ball can pass through the arches easily. Arrange the arches in a playing course like the one shown on the next page.

How to play spoonball:

The object of the game is to hit your ball from Goal A, through the course, around Goal B, and back to Goal A.

Start at Goal A. Take turns hitting. You must hit the ball through at least one arch on every hit. If you miss an arch, you lose the turn. Leave your ball where it is.

If you go through the arch, you get another hit. Keep hitting until you miss an arch.

You get a point every time you go around Goal B or return to Goal A.

Start here

Goal A

Goal B

INDIANS | PILGRIMS

Measurements

If you should need to find out the metric values of measurements given in these projects, this chart will help:

1 inch	=	25.4 millimeters
1 foot	=	30.5 centimeters
1 teaspoon	=	5 milliliters
1 tablespoon	=	14.8 milliliters
1 cup	=	.24 liter